LOVE IS THE RESCUE

LOVE
is the
RESCUE

Patti Raggets

LUMINARE PRESS
WWW.LUMINAREPRESS.COM

Love is the Rescue
Copyright © 2024 by Patti Raggets

All rights reserved. This book or any portion thereof may not be reproduced or used in any manner whatsoever without the express written permission of the publisher, except for the use of brief quotations in a book review.

Printed in the United States of America

Luminare Press
442 Charnelton St.
Eugene, OR 97401
www.luminarepress.com

LCCN: 2024911154
ISBN: 979-8-88679-598-1

*To my mother, Mary. Your words of wisdom
and actions of support live on in my heart
and are what carry me through.*

---

*It is time we open our hearts to love,
stop protecting ourselves from pain,
and make the love transparent in life.
Let your love shine as God's love shines on us.
Even in the darkest of days
the sun always shines!*

Love, Patti

Table of Contents

Goblin 3

Caged Animal 16

Bitterness to Betterness 27

Install New Programming 38

A Pearl Made From Grit 58

Spiral Jetty 77

Acknowledgements 83

"Educating the mind without educating the heart is no education at all."

"Aristotle"

GOBLIN

It felt like I was a million miles away.

Darkness surrounded me. In the distance came a woman's voice calling my name, "Patti, Patti, Patti, stay with us!"

Slowly, the fog of my blackout lifted. My son, George, would later say it had been the longest minute and a half of his life.

He had watched as my tongue stuck out, my face turned ghostly white, and my eyes rolled in the back of my head. I did not appear to be breathing, and it was a struggle to find a pulse with all the warm clothing I had on.

I had no response to outside stimulation, even as George and his girlfriend frantically pulled my hair and slapped me in the face, George desperately screaming, "Mom, wake the FUCK UP!"

It was President's Day in February of 2019 at Goblin Valley State Park. I was on my annual trip from Ohio to Utah to spend time with my oldest son, George. I was hiking with George, his girlfriend, Taylor, and their dog, Kota, when we found ourselves in the nastiest of conditions. It had been snowing, and the mixture of sand and dirt created a slopping mess of mud as the temperatures started to rise throughout the early afternoon.

A tremendous amount of mud had started to build up on my boots. I took a step down and heard a *snap!* Within seconds, I realized it had been the sound of my own ankle breaking. I matter-of-factly announced this to my son and his girlfriend, then promptly fell unconscious.

After his panicked attempts to awaken me, my son was beside himself with relief when I finally came to. Shifting his focus now that I was awake, he began to worry about how he could get me help. We were easily an hour outside of any cell phone reception. The ranger station was closed on President's Day, we had not seen another hiker all day, and the weather conditions were only worsening.

My son's first idea was to leave me behind in his survival blanket with water and snacks while he went with his girlfriend for help.

"What kind of help?" I asked at this suggestion.

"A helicopter," he said.

"Please, do not leave me here alone! I will crawl out of here before you leave me here alone!" I begged.

I was unable to walk, my ankle limp and dangling from my leg.

"Do you have a better idea?" he grimly replied.

"We can ask God to send some angels to help us." I spoke.

Frustrated, he snapped, "Mom, this is not the time for your spiritual shit!"

"No," I countered, "this is the time we need it the most!" I went forth and prayed, "God, please send some angels to help us."

God wasted no time at all answering my cry. Within minutes, a small group of people came into our frame of view. From our vantage point, they were rising straight out of the earth, like actors being lifted from a trap room up to the front and center of a Broadway stage.

The sun started to shine for the first time all day. I knew it was God shining his light on all of us. The angels he sent us in human form were three strong young men and five brave young women. I asked everyone to take a moment to thank God for showing up.

I wrapped Kota's dog leash around my wrist and under my knee to hold up my leg. The guys carried me up like a chair as the girls went ahead to find the easiest path out.

After carrying, crawling, and hobbling through gullies in the thickest of mud for over a mile, we finally managed to get to the car. Before parting, I asked my son to get a contact number for these angels on earth. I insisted on giving each of them a hug and thanking them.

After driving for an hour, we stopped at a Subway in a gas station where there was cell service. My son's girlfriend went in to get ice. She came out with a bag to put on my foot. It said "Muchas Gracias"—(thank you)—on the bag. I remember thinking, okay *God, you must be asking me to do something* and a sense of peace washed over me.

I refused to beat myself up over this accident and focused all my energy on moving forward. I called my insurance company and talked to a nurse. She told me where to find the closest Urgent Care, which was one and a half hours away from Moab, Utah.

Not only was Urgent Care an additional hour and a half out of the way from my son's home in Salt Lake City, but I was also concerned that Urgent Care would not be equipped to help with an injury of my severity.

Suspecting the nurse's answer already, I asked, "What are my other options?"

"Drive three hours to Salt Lake City to the hospital," she replied.

Despite the daunting length of time in the car, I knew that heading to the University of Utah Hospital in Salt Lake City with its level one trauma center was a much better use of our time.

As we set out in the car for the hospital, I could see the shock still etched on my son and his girlfriend's faces. I could feel their lingering terror from watching me go unconscious, not knowing if I would come to. I wanted to lighten the mood and started cracking jokes at them.

My son gave me the whole back seat with their dog bed and blankets to prop my foot on, and I found myself to be extremely comfortable with this setup. As a mom, I could not help but worry about my son and his girlfriend, especially as I watched her legs go numb from carrying 45-pound Kota on her lap in the front seat. Shifting my focus to them also helped distract my mind from the relentless pain in my ankle.

After three long hours, we finally arrived at the University of Utah Hospital Emergency Room. X-Rays revealed that two bones were confirmed broken, my fibula and tibia, the bones that hold my ankle to my leg. They told me I would need to have surgery involving a plate and ten screws.

I was not sure what to do, so the doctors splinted my ankle and gave me it until the next morning to decide whether to have the surgery done there in Utah or back home in Ohio. It was getting late, and I was growing so uncomfortable in the sweaty, muddy clothes still clinging to my skin. When I asked if I could have a pair of scrubs to change into, the nurses said they would have to cut my leggings off like they had done for my boot and sock. Those were my most favorite pair of leggings, so I asked if two nurses could hold each side of the pants and stretch them wide around the ankle instead of cutting them off. I took a deep breath and held it the whole time. It hurt like no other, but they got it done.

Finally, discharged at 12:30 a.m. and went back to my son's house. It was time to decide in the morning if I would be heading to the airport or going under the knife. I called my husband, George Senior, who pledged his support with whatever I would decide.

My son weighed in with his opinion that I would have a much stronger support system back in Ohio. If I had the surgery in Utah, I would not be able to fly home for weeks due to the blood thinners. I decided that he was right.

I chose to stay in Utah until my scheduled flight home in a couple of days. In these days of waiting before flying home, my son made the couch so comfortable to rest and sleep on. George does quite a bit of camping, he had many sizes and varieties of pillows, a foam mattress, and blankets. George made the best breakfast for me each morning. We enjoyed each other's company throughout the day, alternating between spending the time in conversation and binge watching the Netflix show "*Somebody Feed Phil,*" to provide us with very relaxing entertainment.

We even found the time for me to cut his hair the night before I left. Being a professional hair stylist, I found it comical that his favorite haircut of all time from me was while I was sitting down. I used this time that we had together while I was cutting his hair to assure him that my broken ankle was not his fault. I sensed that he felt responsible, and I hoped I was able to convince him to let go of that burden.

Before leaving, George set me up well with an impressive pair of crutches. They had a rounded foot at the bottom instead of those ones with a stump. He searched multiple stores before finding the perfect ones.

On the ride to the airport, a great sadness enveloped me as I pictured the long recovery that lay ahead. I was especially sad not knowing how long it would be before I would be well enough to return for a visit. I really treasure my time out in Utah, always so full of fun and new adventures beyond my imagination. On this 2019 trip, my son had wanted to show me the rest of Utah's mighty five National Parks along with the state parks and the hidden gems that very few people know about in Southern Utah. We had made it to Corona Arch, Canyon Lands, Delicate Arch, and Little Wild Horse Slot Canyons in San Rafael Swell before I had my accident at Goblin Valley and our plans were derailed.

I shook off my disappointment at all we were not able to do on this trip, and let my mind wander back to our multitude of past Utah adventures. We hiked up mountains in the snow to sled back down them on a *Euroseld Merikan Missile Sled*—a sled with a high-performance design that allows for fast turning with handles to hold for stability to allow for all the winter fun. We went into the stunning backcountry behind Deer Valley Ski Resort to snowmobile, snowshoe, cross country ski, and with my son's patient guidance, to downhill ski.

I thought back on that first successful downhill skiing attempt. I had been thinking to myself—, *just be like Lindsey Vonn!*—hoping that holding the vision of the great American Alpine Olympic downhill skier would empower me to make it down the mountain. I had been so scared at the top, filled with a deep fear that led to a full-blown meltdown. —I cannot do this!" I cried. But with my son's help and my visualization of Lindsey Vonn's Olympic run, I triumphed! That feeling of success was amazing.

Remembering the elation of that first downhill ski served as a stark contrast to my current malfortune. I brought myself back into the present as I said a tearful goodbye to George.

I was a little scared to fly alone, but I found Delta Air Lines to be so helpful. The flight attendant said she had once suffered a similar injury, and kindly stacked beverage boxes on top of each other to help me prop my leg up. She asked multiple people in first class if they would give up their pillows to make my makeshift stool more comfortable, and they all acquiesced. In my row, a lady shared that she had also broken her ankle last year and offered to assist if I needed anything. I felt comforted and protected in the empathetic presence of those who knew exactly what I was experiencing.

The flight went more quickly than I had imagined. I was traveling alone with a tremendous number of heavy emotions not knowing the next time I would be able to travel and visit my son. In fact, the waiting period to be the last person to get off the flight to accommodate my injury felt longer than the actual flight itself!

The last guy to get off the plane before me stopped, wished me good luck, and assured me that I would be back hiking again soon.

"Those of us who hike out west have it written in our souls to get back out there," he said. I felt encouraged by his message.

The woman who assisted me in getting off the plane was so nice and helpful. As she was pushing the wheelchair, she asked who was picking me up. I told her my husband and youngest son were. When I finally saw George Senior and my son, Austin, all the anxiety I had been carrying completely went away.

Arriving at home, I saw that George Senior and Austin had turned my home office into a bedroom for me, so I was able to sleep on the first floor. Even though everything was on the first floor, it still seemed so hard to get around having to bear all my weight on one leg. The crutches were wearing my arms out!

The next morning, I had an appointment with orthopedic surgeon Doctor Adam Miller from Beacon Orthopedics. *How can you go wrong following a beacon?* I smiled to myself, seeing a sign of hope in the name.

I peppered him with a barrage of questions—"Where did you study? What do you do on the weekends? Do you drink? Will you be hungover on Monday for surgery?"

He remained so calm, confident, and collected, even when I shared that I could have had this surgery done by a surgeon in Utah who studied in Switzerland and works on Olympians.

He let me know that he has a two-year-old and that his wife is pregnant with their second child, so he did not do much of anything on the weekends. He then asked me if my hair salon clients drill me about hair like I drilled him with questions about surgery.

"Of course they do," I said. "It's their appearance we're talking about!"

On the way home from the meeting, my husband said, "Wow, you sure did drill that doctor!"

"I was looking to see if he would respond defensively. But he stayed calm and collected, showing me that he is confident in knowing who he is and that he knows his job well. He did not flinch at any of the questions I asked him. I needed to see that, being that HE'S the one that was going to perform the surgery on my ankle, and it is my foot!" I shared.

After arriving home, it was time to prepare for surgery. Not only did I have to take a blood thinner, but I also had to get a shot in the abdomen, and holy cow that hurt like hell! It was challenging to get around on one foot. My life was completely thrown off balance, and tomorrow would mark step one towards getting it back.

Goblin Reflection Questions

1. Do you trust and believe in a higher power? What experiences do you have where you have felt the presence of this higher power?

2. Do you visualize a positive or negative outcome in stressful situations?

3. Do you honor your anxiety and fear to learn from it? Do you know you can use it for your good?

4. Are you able to sit with the feelings of fear to go beyond it and see what it can teach you?

5. What do you do to balance the inner "Goblins" in your head when you find yourself experiencing negative thoughts?

6. Do you feel confident asking questions and being an advocate for yourself?

CAGED ANIMAL

I had never felt so helpless, weak, and vulnerable in my entire life. The pain was excruciating, and the post-op blood thinner shots were weakening both my body and my mind.

The doctor told me that my surgery had gone well, and thanks to the nerve blockers, I was feeling well, too. Little did I know I would be in a world of pain a couple of days later as the nerve blockers wore off.

In the waiting room, my entire body filled with anxiety. I had felt like just another face in the crowd when the first nurse led me back to prepare to go under the knife.

"Put these on, lie down on the table, and someone will be back to take your vitals," she commanded, tossing a pair of scrubs my way, and swiftly marching back out the door.

The next nurse came in shortly after to take my blood pressure and start my IV. She tied the rubber band around my arm so tightly that it felt like my arm would snap in two!

Neither of the nurses introduced themselves, nor did they take the time to explain exactly what they were going to do. While for them it was just another ordinary day at work, for me this was anything but.

I felt a greater need for human connection. Even something as simple as introducing themselves by name would have done wonders to put me more at ease. The mind-body connection is powerful, and I wanted to be prepared on all fronts for my surgery.

The surgery team came out to wheel me back into the OR. The anesthesiologist placed an oxygen mask on my face, and after jokingly warning me that it would smell like a plastic beach ball, told me to count backwards from ten.

I was out and back awaking in the blink of an eye.

My first thought upon waking after surgery was, *hmm that was not so bad…but my foot does look a little crooked.*

I was handed a couple of crackers and a cup of water, then told to go home.

Being that it was an outpatient procedure, my husband was able to drive me back home right away. It was nightfall by the time we got back home. I took my pain meds and went to sleep.

The next morning, he greeted me with a delicious breakfast. The aroma of bacon and coffee filled the room. I enjoyed this lovingly prepared breakfast in bed from my husband, grateful for his tender care.

This was the first of many meals that he would go on to prepare for me as I recovered, including some particularly memorable breakfasts like a bowl of oatmeal complete with berries and pecans carefully arranged to make a smiley face and a plate with eggs for eyes, tomatoes for cheeks, avocadoes for eyebrows, and a big bacon smile. My sweet husband filled up not only my stomach, but also my heart with these kind and creative gestures.

Two days later, the nerve block wore off. Holy Cow…more like Holy F**K! The pain radiated in every fiber of my being. I begged my husband to help me find a way to get any form of relief.

He called the doctor, and I was thankfully prescribed Oxycodone. However, their offices close early so my son, Austin, had to drive clear across town to pick it up from another provider.

When Austin finally returned with my prescription, I had my first taste of sweet relief. Unfortunately, that relief was short-lived. While the Oxycodone did nullify my pain, it also brought on a slew of side effects.

I felt the urge to pee, yet I was completely unable to urinate. I felt delirious. My body was achingly stiff and atrophying from needing to be so still all the time. I felt so restless. I was also taking a nightly blood thinner shot, which made me feel weak in both mind and body. My vision was blurry, like seeing through Saran Wrap.

Oxycodone, blood thinners, and the inability to move combined like a dark force taking over my body. Prior to this injury, I had always been reluctant to take even a Tylenol or Ibuprofen, let alone a cocktail of powerful drugs like this.

I found myself trapped in a vicious cycle. Forgoing the meds and the pain relief they brought simply was not an option. The unmedicated pain was truly unbearable. It felt like a chainsaw, electric screwdriver, and a fencing sword were all going through my ankle at the same time. The nerve pain shooting through my entire body felt like I was connected up to an electrical current.

I took to calling 8 p.m., the time for my nightly blood thinner shot, my witching hour. One night as my husband was preparing my shot, the movie "*Bridget Jones's Baby*" was playing on TV. There was a scene where she got an amniocentesis done to determine paternity.

As I watched the fifteen-inch needle inserted into her abdomen, boy, did I shift into gratitude that my needle was only two inches long! While the two-inch needle still caused me significant pain, the visual contrast from that scene gave me a much-needed perspective.

This whole experience was proving to be so much more challenging than I could have ever anticipated. The nights dragged on and on. At times it felt like an entire month had passed in the duration of a single night. Winter in Ohio means darkness early in the evening and late into the morning. While, I was so accustomed to these dark winters, it was the first time I had ever experienced such a darkness of the soul.

Eight long months passed, and while I was nowhere near my regular energy level, I finally had the pain management in a place where I could return to the salon. I emailed my clients to let them know I was coming back to work. Little did I know that my healing journey was about to take another detour.

Moments after sending the email, I got a call from a nurse practitioner. On top of everything else I was going through; a mysterious ear infection had started plaguing me for months on end. She had ordered a blood test to try to get at the root of what was going on.

My bloodwork revealed extremely concerning results. My white blood cell count was so low that she thought I might need a blood transfusion.

She referred me to a hematologist, whose analysis shifted everything into place. It turned out that I was allergic to the stainless-steel plates and screws in my ankle from surgery! He recommended that I have another surgery immediately to get them back out.

I was extremely excited. It was a relief to know that a tangible solution for long term pain relief was on the horizon at last.

The morning of the surgery, I woke up incredibly early to go work out, because I knew it would be a while before I would be able to again. Having to wait to work out again felt like I was going backward. I had finally started to gain momentum and it felt like I would now be starting back on day one.

The surgery went quickly, only 35 minutes long. I thanked God that there were no blood thinners this time around.

I was in a boot for two weeks, which meant I was back on crutches and a knee scooter. The incision was very painful to put weight on, so I opted not to move much until I went -to my first post-op appointment. The darkness that I had just fought my way out of for so long descended back upon me at once.

To boost my mood, my friend Teri Lynn offered her beautiful home as a gift for rest and relaxation. So, my husband planned a ten-day trip to Palm Springs, California. It was beautiful. Palm trees swayed against the backdrop of a bright blue sky. I felt the sunshine seep into my very soul. It was also a great relief to my ankle, which was now sensitive to temperature due to the surgeries.

After an amazing trip, it was time to return home. On our flight back, the man seated behind me was coughing up a storm. My stomach pooled with dread; very much consumed with anxiety wondering how I could avoid his germs in such a tight, enclosed space. Sure enough, shortly after we arrived back home, I came down with a sore throat, fever, and headache.

I had to stay home from work to sleep and rest. My immune system had weakened not only from having that metal in my body for so long, but also from having yet another surgery done to get it back out. All throughout the holiday season I continued to struggle with my health. I just felt so tired and worn down. My mental health plummeted again as I lacked the energy to fully participate in all the holiday festivities that brought me joy.

When friends stopped by, I had put on a front that I was good. I did not want them really knowing what was really going on in my mind. I was feeling the crushing weight of depression. It felt like I was at the bottom of a dark hole, desperate to see even one ray of light.

The depression was a dark, stormy cloud that refused to leave. My mind felt trapped inside of a rain cloud, and the walls were closing in on me. I had never in my life been so emotionally, physically, and spiritually drained. I was so desperately sad and defeated that no matter what I tried to accomplish, it took me forever to get around.

For someone so used to doing things fast, this new snail's pace was unbearable.

I had a whole new understanding for anyone who has ever been depressed. I realized that I had harbored a sense of judgment for those I have seen struggling with their mental health. As someone always naturally drawn to the light and seeing the best in any circumstance, I never understood what it meant to be so low and so down that finding the light just seemed impossible.

I tried hard to pull myself out of the dark days. There were days I would just sit with a vacant stare, not even wanting to watch TV. I was waiting and waiting for any type of light to enter, for relief from my mental and physical anguish.

There was even a night where I contemplated just ending it all. It felt like my power center, the very core of who I am, had just gone out. The excruciating pain with no foreseeable end in sight had taken a powerful grip on my very being.

I stared at the open bottles of Oxycodone and Hydrocodone on my nightstand. I imagined consuming all the remaining pills at once to finally put an end to my pain. I thought of my family. In my dark and desperate state, I truly felt they would be better off without me, as burdensome as I had become.

It was the lowest I had ever been in my life. I so wanted to end the pain not only from the plate and screws in my ankle, but also the pain of feeling so caged in like an animal.

I was so down; completely sunk into a level of deep darkness I had never experienced in my life. My body was becoming unrecognizable, and even more concerning, so was my spirit. I am usually the one who can shift a conversation from dark to light in a nanosecond! But every thought coursing through me was disturbingly dark and negative. I found myself truly not wanting to exist anymore.

Suddenly, my mind brought forward the faces of two dear friends. One, who had lost a brother to suicide. The other, whose husband was fighting hard to live another day while waiting for a double organ transplant. I pictured their anger and despair at me choosing to end my own life. As impossible as it seemed, I knew I had to keep trying to pull myself out of the darkness.

Caged Animal Reflection Questions

1. Isolation can create a tremendous amount of depression. Do you have a list of contacts you can reach out for help to get you out of it?

   _____
   _____
   _____

2. Do you allow yourself to be vulnerable?

   _____
   _____
   _____

3. Do you know it is healthy to allow people to help you when you need assistance? Do you struggle asking for help when you need it?

   _____
   _____
   _____

4. Are you aware of the effects that narcotics can have on your mental health?

   _____
   _____
   _____

5. Do you reach out to family and friends and offer if they need anything during a difficult or challenging time?

_____
_____
_____

BITTERNESS TO BETTERNESS

Father Ruffino is a Ugandan priest who lives here in Cincinnati preaching at Combonian Missionaries. I went to meet with him after a recommendation from a client of mine.

Speaking with him felt like I had a line straight to God's ear! An aura of peace radiated all around him.

During our visit, I poured out all my pent-up frustration about my ankle and multiple number of setbacks and difficulties I had been facing on my healing journey. He listened attentively, taking in all I had to say. After I finished unloading my stream of consciousness on him, he paused for a moment, then shared something I would never forget.

"Patti," he said. "Can you turn your bitterness to betterness?"

My bitterness to betterness, I mused. I liked the sound of that.

He then placed his hands directly on my head for a couple of minutes and then on my ankle.

"Your ankle will be okay," he said. "It is just not

done yet." You still have quite a bit of emotional, spiritual, and physical pain you need to heal."

Walking out of our meeting, I felt the deepest sense of peace. It really felt like God was directly touching me.

I thought back to a time that I collaborated with another spiritual teacher. My friend, a healer named Blu, was brought to tears as she worked on me. She cried, saying how I was not properly nurtured as a young child. Her words resonated. Being the youngest of five, I felt very overlooked.

I then thought back to my experience starting school. The school identified me as being "slow," and put in a class for "slow learners." My senior year of high school, my guidance counselor told me directly that I was "too stupid" for college.

I can now see that being told I was slow had made me want to run, and fast! So run I did! I used my mother's inheritance money to start my own hair salon and I never looked back. When I became a wife and a mother, I kept charging forward. Working, caring for my family, cooking, cleaning, giving so much to everyone but myself.

All of that running seemed to be serving me, but looking back I can see the resentment that had started to slowly fester over time. I had been figuratively running at the speed of light to disprove the narrative that I was slow, so when my life slowed down, I was forced to stop and look at what exactly I was running from.

I was in a race to prove myself, a race that was brought to a screeching halt due to my injury. So much of my bitterness stemmed from my inability to do things for myself. I had no choice but to take a step back. What I did not realize was that this would create the opportunity for my loved ones to step up.

My husband was able to stay home from work to care for me for three and a half weeks after my first surgery. I wondered how he felt as I watched all the chores that I typically do fall on him. From grocery shopping and cooking—including making sunny side eggs for the first time in his life, to cleaning and laundry, to running all errands and taking charge of all my doctor's appointments. Watching him capably step up to meet my needs made me realize that being in touch with and voicing my needs was something that I needed to do more of.

When my husband had to return to work, my next full-time caregiver stepped up. My sister-in-law Kathy arrived for ten days to take over the reins. She was such an incredible help and joyful spirit to have around. She did everything! She organized all my things that had become strewn all over the house in the wake of my injury. She even made my husband's favorite sticky buns, homemade cinnamon rolls with pecans and gooey glaze dripping all over it. The aroma of smelling those rolls baking first thing on a Sunday morning filled me to my soul.

Kathy and my husband get along so well. They cracked jokes with each other every day. They started joking with me, calling me The Princess.

"What do you think The Princess wants today for dinner?" they would say.

This lighthearted joke caused a profound shift in my thinking. Instead of a helpless patient burdening her family, I could now see myself as a treasured princess, worthy of being waited on hand and foot.

After a week, the thought hit me, *wait: if I am the princess, who is the queen?* I voiced the thought to Kathy who laughed and said that it was her, since she is taking care of me!

Kathy effortlessly incorporated humor into her loving and nurturing. It was common for her to greet me in the morning saying, "Get your sorry ass out of bed, you act like you have a broken ankle or something!"

She never failed to get a laugh out of me. I absolutely loved our time together. We started off every day talking, crying, and laughing. We called it our therapy time. Then she would spend the rest of the day productive in getting things done for me.

When Kathy left, so many other friends stepped up to help my royal treatment continue. After weeks of sponge bathing, my legs were so prickly. It felt like I had gone camping for months! I found myself praying for a real shower, to feel truly clean again.

My prayer answered in the form of my friend, Sally, who called and offered to take me to our gym to use the handicap showers. She was so incredibly patient in assisting with helping with my foot and leg.

She helped me scrub the doctor's initials off where he had written in pen on my leg. It felt so amazing to wash that visual reminder of that painful day down the drain. The shower not only cleaned me physically, but also felt like it had washed a layer of darkness off me as well.

My friends were simply amazing. They rallied and brought dinners for ninety straight days! Most people only bring food for a couple of days or weeks after an incident. My friends kept the food coming for so long that I eventually had to ask them to stop! The love they conveyed in cooking and delivering for me left me feeling full physically and spiritually.

The support of loved ones like these friends and my family was the only thing that could lift my spirits. I have always believed that no one truly walks alone in this world. I have a faith in a higher power, which may go by multiple names, but who I call God.

In the darkest of times, I always knew that I was never alone. Multiple times, I called out, and every time I heard an answer. Oftentimes, that answer was in the form of my family and friends continuing to show up for me repeatedly. I truly thank God for my friends that were reaching out and so supportive. It sure is what kept me charging forward.

I had so many offers to take me to lunch and coffee dates. My friend, Teri, called asking if she could pick me up to take me to her home for lunch. She went out of her way to pick me up, to take me to her home, and drop me off.

I remember going into her beautiful home, seeing the table set all with the food on it in the kitchen. She had plated a beautiful lunch, arranged in an almost artistic way. There was chicken salad on bibb lettuce with other veggies to accompany it, homemade tea with blackberries and oranges floating in it, and a side dish of cheese, jam, and crackers to nibble on.

Once again, I felt like The Princess. After lunch, we went to her screened-in porch and had the best conversation about love. Surrounded by dozens of cardinals in her backyard, the sun was shining, the skies were blue, and the temperature was a perfect 72 degrees. It was truly a wonderful day of food and friendship.

Lunch and coffee dates like these were wonderful for keeping my body moving and giving me a reason to look forward to getting up in the morning. I felt motivated to get myself dressed, put makeup on, and do my hair. That helped me to feel pretty despite my continued pain.

All these loved ones who reached out to help take me places, cook food, assist in sponge bath set ups, take me on lunch outings or coffee dates, bring me dinner after dinner, all filled my heart with so much love. I especially enjoyed the way this deepened each relationship and allowed me to get to know each person in a more intimate way.

One of my clients, Sudie, is 96 years old. She called me up one day.

"Patti," she began. "Remember when I broke my ankle when I was 90 and I needed 24-hour care for 6 months?"

She told me that I would survive this injury. That I may not be happy during the process, but that I would survive.

"You can call me anytime," she reassured me. I felt soothed and empowered by her words.

In a twist of fate, my daughter-in-law, Sarah, had suffered an injury only days before I did, fracturing her elbow in a ninja move. Even as she was navigating her own healing journey, she still took time daily to check in with me and send positivity my way. I told her she was a light worker because of the love and compassion she has for others. The light she sends out is right from her heart. She really is a true inspiration to me. She has been there for me in the past when I felt like I had not one person to turn to who utterly understands being so low.

The year before, she and my son, Austin, had given me a bracelet made of rose quartz to represent love, wood to represent courage, and hematite to represent harmony. On days when I really wanted to give up, looking down at my wrist and thinking of them helped motivate me to keep going.

I reflected on the years leading up to my injury. I realized that in the last five years, I had been so emotionally drained, constantly feeling like I was giving so much and receiving so little in return.

Just as Father Ruffino had said, there was more than a broken ankle that needed to heal. I was giving and giving to everyone but myself. My heart was hurting and showing signs of pure exhaustion. This healing journey showed me that when you do not listen to your own body, nature will force you to.

As frustrating as my limitations were during my recovery, I really do feel that I needed a respite. I was seriously exhausted with nothing left to give. The rest really cleared my lungs and soothed the accelerated rhythm of my heartbeat. It gave me a much-needed break from the stress and demands of others' needs. The rest also showed me the amount of help I really do have around me if I step back and allow myself to receive it.

The way I was living my life was out of control, but it took losing total control for me to see it. I learned that I do not need to be a patient to receive the same treatment as a princess.

Bitterness to Betterness Reflection Questions

1. How well do you listen when someone is in need?

   _____
   _____
   _____

2. Do you offer compassion and love or judgment when someone is hurting?

   _____
   _____
   _____

3. Have you ever explored the idea of seeking a healer or different modalities to help you heal and feel better?

   _____
   _____
   _____

4. Do you feel worthy of love? How well do you love and accept yourself?

   _____
   _____
   _____

5. How do you push past limiting beliefs?

6. Do you find yourself noticing the signs and wonders on Earth?

INSTALL NEW PROGRAMMING

I was stuck. I was in my car, ready to tackle the day's appointments, when my car refused to start. I was so bewildered.

What was up with my car? I thought. *It is the beginning of August. Why will my car not start?*

This car was new! Purchased two years ago with only 19,000 miles in it. I called for roadside assistance. Two hours later, they arrived and told me the problem was with my battery. They had jumped my car battery, then told me to let it run for 20 minutes afterwards. I did, but it was still running slowly for the rest of the day.

The next day, I could barely get my ignition turned over. I called Subaru, who told me to bring it in to get serviced. They told me that I needed a new battery, and new programming to help keep the battery recharging.

"Ma'am, it's best if you get some freeway driving in," the technician said. "Are you scared to go onto the freeway?" he asked.

"No," I laughed, "I am not afraid to go onto the freeway! I broke my ankle, and I only travel to rehab, the gym, and the grocery store."

He said my car registered only short distance driving over the last five months and told me that I need to drive more than two-mile stretches.

OH MY GOD! I thought. I have been living my life in a two-mile radius! Me, the girl who loves adventures and travel and seeing and learning new things! I have become an old lady at 53-years old!

I have always believed that age is just a number, that we are as we allow ourselves to think we are. I always loved and prioritized keeping my childlike-self alive. It is the part of us that creates all the fun!

When I got home, I took a good look at myself in the mirror. *WOW, this injury really has taken a toll on me,* I thought. *I look worn out!* I reflected further on my physical condition. *I walk with a limp, my skin looks old, and I am in the worst shape of my life.* I lamented.

Even though I had been going to the gym, it was suggested that I take it slow. And slow is not my speed! My brain works fast. I walk fast. People have always said that I walk like a girl on a mission. It takes so much patience to adjust to moving slower. It felt like I was losing myself.

Feeling slow is particularly triggering for me. I was placed in school in the "slow" learner classes growing up, the word SLOW has been in my programming my whole life. I realized that I needed to heal this wound, to learn that my identity should never be tied together with the pace at which I am living life.

The man's recommendation was to drive on the freeway. I also needed to be free! Free from the emotional pain continuing to weigh me down, free from carrying the judgments of others. To drive the way to free myself of all the pain that has had my body feeling stuck my whole life.

Just as my car needed new programming alongside its new battery, I was also in need of new programming! I was tired, hardly turning over a new lease in life. I was dying to myself on the inside, and I needed to make a shift before my own battery ran out completely.

Multiple teachers appeared to help me reprogram. I worked with Healing Touch practitioners, Reiki experts, intuitivist, acupuncturists, mind coaches, and emotional healers who deal strictly with pent up emotions. Each healer I went to helped heal a different layer of pain. All the parts of my mind, spirit, and physical body needed healing. The dark was buried so deep into my core.

After months of seeing diverse types of healers each week, the light started pouring into me. I learned how to release one layer at a time, understanding that without true surrender and release, the dark would always have a hold on me.

During one healing appointment I heard very loudly, *ALL RESENTMENT IS NOW LEAVING YOUR BODY. IT IS GONE!*

I had been carrying so much resentment for so long. My whole life I have been an active person, enjoying working out, and any array of outdoor activities. I built up so much resentment when it felt like there was no end in sight for my injury, when I could not even conjure up an image of the future me walking, being active, enjoying hiking, biking, working out or swimming. It was so hard for me to not be able to move my body in the ways I always did. I felt so vulnerable, like I had nothing to give even to myself.

I felt like I had brought home many inner goblins after that fateful day in Goblin Valley State Park. These inner goblins lived inside my brain. The darker they became, the meaner I felt. I found myself hating people and being so mad at everything. I was especially bitter about the people who stayed silent and made no effort to help me at all.

There were several people who you think will be there for you. Seeing the level of compassion that really exists out there was sad to me. How could I open myself up to those who really do not care? I felt very angered by it all, not wanting to forgive.

It sent me into a judgmental place, feeling vindictive, never wanting to offer my help to them in the future. It made me want to run away, move, start a new life. It was wild how these goblins pushed these few people into the forefront of my mind, banishing the thoughts of the dozens of loved ones who were there for me at every step of the way.

Next, I heard,—"*You are free to focus on peace, love and joy.*"—I realized these resentful thoughts were an attempt at self-protection, a way for me to guard my heart. But what I really needed was to open myself up to love and release all the resentment. When I was able to do so in the session, I felt the strongest rush of peace and joy. I was able to release the anger of this situation and see the true gifts in all of it.

Feeling the energy releasing all that pain has created such a calming effect to be able to stay clear and focused on my path and purpose. Releasing the power of surrender of trust to believe that all the details of life really do take care of themselves. Releasing the need to control is the true ticket to surrendering. I had to release that before the healing could take place and enter my body. Holding onto it was not serving me.

My spirits had been so dampened that it was evident even to those who had not even known me before my injury! At a follow-up with my surgeon after multiple weeks in physical therapy, he gave me the best news, news that had felt like it was never going to come in my darkest of times. In six months,' time, I would finally be free to resume my life to the fullest! The elation must have been quite evident on my face.

"Patti, that's the first time I've seen your light on!" he said.

His words called to mind a favorite quote, "When someone's light is out, we have the ability to reignite someone else's by just shining our light onto them." That is exactly what my doctor did for me at that moment. I smiled thinking of the name of the practice—"Beacon Orthopedics"— and how they gave me a beacon of light! There is no greater gift than the gift of light.

My body still ached all over from the atrophy of lying around so much, I knew movement would help me feel whole again. I just knew it was not who I am to continue to just sit around and do nothing. I had to get my body moving again, I felt weak, and I knew I was the one that needed to take charge of my life.

I hired a trainer, Jonathan, to help me. Jonathan is a certified mental coach, specializing in mental toughness. He gave me a warrior band for my wrist, saying that every time I have a doubt, feel fear, or want to give up, to give it a quick snap on my wrist.

He then gave a great piece of advice that he had received from a baseball coach when he was young. "You can be a marshmallow, an M&M, or a rock. Mentally, will you turn to ash fast, crack open and melt, or be strong like a rock?"

Those analogies just felt like gifts wrapped up in hope. There is something about the gym that can help restore so many broken parts of the spirit, mind, and body. Working so diligently and getting into a small routine again helps the mind move forward. I joke around saying I have always had a chubby looking appearance and the only thing that was skinny on my body was my ankles. It was so tough to push through the pain because I could feel the hardware in my ankle with no cushion to help alleviate the pain. I felt so challenged by every move I made.

I learned that I needed to start looking for small wins. To restart my brain, which had been stuck in so much PTSD and pain, from being so still for so long. Concentrating on my physical triumphs of being able to do the things I love to do needed to be my focus. The gym became a place where I was able to work hard and focus on the small wins, regaining my strength physically, mentally, and spiritually.

I love running into the most random people at the gym. I love seeing people push past their physical limitations, giving me so much inspiration. I especially love reading the messages and quotes on people's shirts. One guy's shirt said, "It's not the size of the dog in the fight, but the size of the fight in the dog." How true is that? I felt encouraged as I fought hard to restore myself.

One day at the gym I ran into Steve, a friend from my Toastmasters group. "Patti, you get a choice to crumble like sandstone or be strong like granite. Will you crumble like sandstone or be strong like granite? Polish it up and SHINE BRIGHTER!" he encouraged.

When I heard that, my spirit immediately felt lighter. I am always seeing signs that bring me to the light, especially on the dark days in my soul that seem so endless. When driving home from the gym one day during a dreary day, I was praying to God. *"Please help restore me back to the light,"* I prayed.

As I approached a traffic light, the car in front of me had a license plate that I had once seen years ago. It said, "4 Earth."

As I saw that plate, I knew God was right there guiding me to know I must stick around.

After a long week of balancing physical therapy, light gym sessions, and working a couple of days, I ran into one of my physical therapists, Sam, while I was out. Going to physical therapy on top of trying to get to the gym and work a couple of days was really starting to take a toll on me.

"How are you doing?" he asked. "I'm really trying to do everything everyone is recommending, and I'm getting very frustrated with my progress," I replied.

He gently reminded me that I had gone through three uncontrolled traumas, and that they would all take time to heal. He explained that orthopedic and musculoskeletal injuries that result from any significant trauma are often associated with PTSD, which can impact the emotional, physical, and functional recovery following an orthopedic procedure.

My intense feelings of frustration, irritability, difficulty concentrating, and insomnia all started to make sense when I reflected on my initial injury, the first surgery, and the follow-up surgery through that lens.

He said, "Healing uncontrolled traumas is one step at a time, one step in front of the next. Nothing on the planet heals us like time! Along with a whole lot of unconditional LOVE!"

I realized that it requires a positive mindset to fully heal. This is not to say that difficult feelings are not meant to be felt and dealt with, for indeed they must! But we cannot stay there, we must allow those feelings to come, and we also must allow them to go.

Achieving a genuinely positive mindset is more than simply telling oneself to think positively. Trying to will oneself into positivity does not work, in fact it often only patches things up and suppresses the real feelings inside.

I took notice of a repeated pattern of sadness sitting in my heart, full of pain. I had to heal each level of pain. Otherwise, it would just continue to come back repeatedly. I had to feel that pain to feel its release.

One morning sitting on the couch, I had put my ankle sideways to see the surgery scar. I ran my hand over the screws and plate in my ankle and started to feel very weird, as if I were going to pass out. My head and ankle hurt badly. A white fog was surrounding me, and I started to become very sweaty and clammy. I called for my husband, and he put a cold compress on my head. While feeling very groggy, I drifted off to sleep.

When I woke up, I had extraordinarily little energy all day long. I just took it easy the rest of the day. The next day I heard intuitively that a layer of trauma from PTSD had left my body. That is not something I can just ignore and wish away. I must work at it one piece at a time. *Finally, a little bit of momentum is gaining! I am moving forward,* I thought.

I saw repeatedly how integrated physical and emotional healing can be. I remember how high my spirits soared as I saw the scar from my second surgery appear. It had taken seven months for the wound scar to heal after my first surgery! Seeing a visual confirmation of physical healing did wonders to heal my emotional state as well.

A major physical clearing I had during my healing journey was a colonoscopy a couple of months after my second surgery. WOW, did I feel so much better afterwards! My eyes, which had been yellowish no matter what I tried, were finally clear and bright. I could feel that the toxins from the surgeries and medicine had finally cleared out! It felt so good to finally feel like I was moving forward.

Before surgery, I remember I looked forward to waking up to be able to enjoy a cup of coffee. As I sipped on my cup of joe, I thought back to a scene from the movie "*Jackie*" that I had watched during my recovery. In the scene, Jackie O. meets with a priest shortly after the death of JFK. She told him how utterly devastated she was to lose her husband, that she felt such despair that she also wanted to die so she could be with him again.

"What about your children, who need you here?" asked the priest. "The pain hurts so bad that not even the children did I want to wake up for," she replied. "Do you drink coffee?" said the priest. "Because if nothing else, there's always a good cup of coffee to wake up for."

Wow! I thought. *What advice from a priest that is!* I thought it must be good enough to have that simple mindset to just wake up for a good cup of joe. When things seem so overwhelmingly hard, absolutely helps to focus on the important things for wins.

One day while I was at a friend's house for tea, I noticed a picture on the wall that was crooked and straightened it. When I got home, I put on a new pair of slippers and noticed the bow on the moccasin was crooked. While lying on the couch, I fixed it to be in the center.

The next day, I had an appointment at Cincinnati Spine and Wellness with Tara, an acupuncturist, to get infrared laser treatments to help heal the surgery wound faster. Tara suggested we also do reflexology and showed me a photo diagram of the left foot. I learned that we receive from the left side of our bodies, and we give out of our right side. I told her that the bottom of my foot had remained numb ever since breaking my ankle. The diagram showed each organ that holds the energies of our feet.

The areas that were still numb showed the heart and brain. My foot, mind, and heart had all been compromised by my accident. We are of mind, body, and soul. Not just an intellectual mind. The heart stores the emotional pain of our lives. We carry the pain with us and tuck it away deep down to protect ourselves from people that seem to enjoy poking those wounds. That is what triggers the pain to never leave.

After my appointment, I went home. Lying on the couch, my foot started really hurting. As though my foot was being manipulated by hands, as if someone was grabbing my ankle and twisting it! The next morning as I woke up, my foot felt like it had shifted into alignment. I heard intuitively, *when your head and heart align, we stop our crooked thinking as in judgements, anger and all emotions that stop us from our core center self.* Then I started hearing lyrics to the song, "Shower the people with LOVE!"

People would remind me that my circumstances were only temporary but believing that while being amid challenging times is easier said than done. I learned to be the owner of this tough time, believing whole-heartedly that it is only temporary. Even when it felt like it would be forever, I started to trust and believe that it would not be.

In our world of instant gratification, I wanted to see the results immediately! But complete results take time. All wounds, like broken bones, require time to mend back together. What really needed mending was my heart. It was sad, with disappointments, lack of confidence, not feeling smart enough to accomplish anything buried deep inside.

All these experiences made me realize that not only did I physically need rescue out of Goblin Valley State Park, but I also needed rescue in my soul. In yoga and meditation, practitioners often talk about quieting our "monkey mind," allowing our thoughts to rest. My "monkey mind" was those goblins in my brain that caused so much of my pain.

I learned that not fully clearing the loads of mental pain along the way in my journey of life allowed for many years of judgment, bitterness, and resentment to catch up with me. I had allowed those feelings to keep me sad and bound up within myself for so long.

Hours upon hours of releasing and letting go brought a deep sense of peace. I automatically shifted into such gratitude. I started seeing things through my childlike self, appreciating the small wins, remembering that bigger is not always better. Sometimes the smallest gestures are the biggest acts of kindness that genuinely reach into your soul. When I can feel that gratitude at a soul level, it makes me come to life as who I really am, appreciating everything I see.

I am so thankful for all the multiple teachers who showed up along the way and guided me to heal the child within that so desperately was screaming for help. That child, who was made to feel she was not smart enough or capable enough on her own, was the source of a deep inner sadness. Feeling abandoned from when I was forced to raise myself because my parents had to work so much to put food on the table. Feeling like I was not ever heard when I spoke. Never feeling smart enough to contribute to conversations. The mindset of *no one wants to hear what you have to say anyway* shuts our voices down and creates blocks upon blocks of closure within. Living in protection within yourself for years thinking *everyone is just going to hurt me*, is a strong belief we create to protect ourselves from having more pain.

Having physical pain at an extraordinarily strong level has helped unveil the real pain I have been carrying around deep inside myself my whole life. I wanted so much more in my life but felt like I never had the answers or inner peace to forge ahead. How could I step forward into being a leader without healing the child within?

Once I recognized what the deep-seated issue was, I was able to healthily heal. It was a powerful energy of healing that needed attention, I relearned how to take the time to rest and do things that make me happy. I carved out time to nurture myself, and it was the best gift I could have given to myself. Simply *being* forced to slow down was the key to a calmer life.

I am surely grateful to have been given this time to finally heal what has truly been the source of my pain my whole life. Instead of only focusing on pleasing others, I learned how to help others when I want to, not because I want to be recognized for doing something good. That is such a different energy, allowing me to feel true joy when helping rather than building resentment. How could one even know the level of joy that truly exists? It had been so long since I had felt such deep, authentic joy within.

I thought back to a conversation I once had with my son. "Why does no one ever notice good character in a person?" he asked me.

"I believe they do," I told him. But why do we wait for someone to give approval? We are really waiting for us to approve of us." I replied.

Until we write our own permission slip to ourselves, we will be living in the pain and misery of waiting for something new to happen. Letting go of the preconceived notions I had about myself allowed me to find total acceptance and approval of myself. When we approve of ourselves, that is when we can truly anchor in feeling worthy, accepted, and loved. We can then go forth with the confidence to be who we came into the world to be.

Until we reach this authentic acceptance of self, we will keep creating situations to repeat the lesson that needed to be learned. It takes courage to do the work within to strengthen your power. Honoring yourself even when you lose sight of the light, it is okay and that we are not meant to stay in that dark place.

Reaching out for help in this process is a necessary and a healthy thing to do. One of my psychologists said, "It's going to be okay." Hearing simple sentences of affirmation like this helps send messages of love to our heart to heal. It is a liberating day when you wake up sharing your gifts to the world by being your authentic self. You can really feel your true colors shining through.

During my healing, I worked on my mind, spirit, and physical body to help me break free from the cage I had created in my mind. I was finally able to instill in myself the confidence and freedom I have been searching for my whole life. No longer would I always strive to please others, always taking a back seat to myself.

One night, I heard the lyrics of the Beatles' song, "Help! Help me if you can, I am feeling down, and I do appreciate your being around. Help me get my feet back on the ground. Won't you please help me?" The song resonated with my soul, which had been screaming out, *someone, help me! Someone, please, come and rescue me!*

It turned out that who I was waiting for all along was my own self. No one else has our unique gifts and purpose. We are here for our own mission to share. I now know to follow and trust my own instincts and signs from the universe because they always lead me in the right direction, even when I think I have gone off course for a while.

I have really grown in touch with my body during this entire process. I have spent countless hours sitting alone amongst the trees and birds on my deck. I feel so peaceful inside my body and am finally in acceptance of who I am. My soul finally aligned while being forced to sit still and allow my body to rest as it needs.

When we do the work to release all of it, is when we are free to be. Being rid of all that pain is a strong feeling of freedom. We know that we are the authors of our own stories, the artists weaving the colors of our own canvas. Shining as bright as the sun, feeling the rainbows as well as seeing them. Building our foundation, with gaining knowledge and wisdom from others to add to our foundation of being our true selves. Powering through!!

Perhaps being out of commission for all this time, was to receive a message of clarity about what to do with my time. Is it a new direction? Something completely different? Will it be clear in the direction? Something that fills my spirit with joy and laughter?

Everything happens for a reason. I was given this time from God to see life in a unique way. To experience what it is like to go slowly, to appreciate the elderly, to gain respect for people that LIVE and deal with physical challenges. To learn to not judge someone who is addicted to pain medication or other drugs, and to have a new level of compassion for those who deal with mental illness.

Until we have walked through a dark place, how can we genuinely appreciate the light? The light we shine out into the world after conquering the darkness is a brighter one. Every day, we get a choice to choose our thoughts. Now I know I can choose the light. I can choose to create a new mindset, new programming.

INSTALLING NEW PROGRAMMING REFLECTION QUESTIONS

1. Is there something you can change about yourself to install new programming?

2. Are you aware that car troubles can reflect what is going on inside of you? What needs repair from the inside out for you?

3. What old wounds can you shed and bring in the light to let go of?

4. What do you do if you feel resentment?

5. What do you know about PTSD? Are you compassionate towards people with mental health challenges?

_____

_____

_____

6. Do you know small gestures can lift someone's spirits? Can you think of a time where you made a gesture like that, or someone made a gesture like that for you?

_____

_____

_____

7. Do you allow time for silence and stillness? How much time do you carve out and allow yourself for fun in nature for self-care?

_____

_____

_____

A PEARL MADE FROM GRIT

One day after watching my family leave the house for work, I felt hit with a powerful wave of envy watching them stride out the door on their own two feet with ease. I felt very trapped, as I was unable to get out of the house without assistance.

My envy turned to depression when I saw the beautiful, blue skied, sunny, and 75-degree day outside the window. I was close enough to see the beautiful day, but unable to go outside and experience it. I felt myself sliding back down into the dark depths of depression.

I decided I could not, would not allow myself to return to that dark place yet again. I decided to take a course of action into my own hands. I managed to get off the couch by rolling towards the floor and catching myself with my hands. Once on the floor, I thought to myself, *I can crawl like babies do…or scoot back using my hands and my right leg…*

When there is a will, there is a way! Someway somehow, I managed to get myself to the sliding glass door, slide it open, and scoot out onto the deck. This one small action felt like the biggest victory, a small step towards creating independence.

I lay in the sunshine on my back, the wooden deck underneath me. God, I love the sun! It just changes everything on a difficult day. When you feel there is no hope, there is always the sun that will lead you to believe otherwise. Putting your face in it can really lift the dark from you. Plus, the color of the sun is so happy. Yellow makes us happy. One of my physical therapists said every time you see a yellow vehicle, think of one thing to be grateful for.

One day I had a follow up appointment with my doctor to start the weight bearing process, and being told that I can start to drive again! As it was my left ankle that had been injured, I still had the use of my driving foot. *Thank God, freedom is in sight!* I thought.

I had to have my husband and son, Austin, go driving with me at first to regain depth perception and confidence. It had been so long since I had driven from being too weak. It was a very weird thing having my son be the one to chaperone my driving!

After a couple of weeks of driving to restore confidence, I went for a drive to drop off invitations to a couple of my friends for the Hats Off Luncheon, a huge philanthropy luncheon for Smale Riverfront Park in Cincinnati. I attended the lunch every year with Sudie, my 96-year-old client. This year, she said she was too old to attend, and told me that I was to take my friends in her stead!

I remember so vividly getting in my car and rolling down the windows, opening the sunroof and blaring the radio. It was my ticket to freedom. I felt like a 16-year-old that just got their license and left the house for the first time without supervision. It was great to feel that rush of independence.

I drove myself to the gym to take an ab class. After class, a woman stopped me and asked, "Why are you here? Lugging that boot around must be so hard, it must weigh a ton to hold one leg up with a boot on." Why was I going to so much trouble just to do a one-legged bridge? She wanted to know.

"Because I'm an athlete," I told her.

"You are?" she said. "What is your sport?"

"Living life to the fullest is my sport," I replied.

She said, "Oh."

I really love receiving invites to unique events for young people. My niece's baby was getting baptized, and the first three rows had reserved signs on them for her family. My husband and I arrived early, being that there were very few parking spots available at the church and I wanted to be able to walk close to the church's entrance. I also wanted to make sure we had an unobstructed view of the baptism.

After finding a seat in the third pew, I noticed a blind couple sitting in the pew behind us. At an angle I was able to see them. They were speaking sweet words to each other and holding hands. It was the sweetest display of love I have seen in a long time.

We were the first of our family to arrive. As increasingly more of our family members joined us, we ended up having to move over across the pew to make room. I wanted to say, "I chose this seat, so I would be able to see!" I was not happy about having to move over.

As the mass progressed, the blind woman proceeded to head towards the podium. She began the first reading so confidently in such a beautiful voice. I thought to myself, *what courage this woman has!* Multiple people are afraid to use their voice in such fear of being judged. Fear of public speaking and the possibility of feeling rejected by others. So, their voices get locked up inside their bodies, like a chain on a bike. Never being heard, their whole lives because this fear is so real. The blind woman just does it! Because she feels called to, she said after mass. Not ever fearing what judgment gets bestowed upon her. Because, as she stood there reading her reading, she spoke to my heart, and I cried; thinking of what beauty we all witnessed by her courage to speak.

Then she approached the podium for the second time and read the petitions, the intentional prayers. She says, "For those who have suffered emotional trauma from an accident…we pray to the Lord."— WOW!!—It was like God was talking to me. Having to move over in the pew, I was in direct alignment of the podium. Those words went straight to my heart, and it felt like a bolt of electric goodness going through it. At that exact moment, the sun came shining right through a gorgeous stain glass window. The sunray came right across my face and shined into my heart. It was such a powerful moment. I thought to myself that God was moving me along the pew exactly where I needed to be to witness such beauty that was healing for my heart.

The blind woman could not see, she just felt it. In that exact moment, the pain left my heart. More profound than a Band-Aid on a wound, as if your heart were being stitched from the inside out. Then, my foot started to feel a release of pain.

The following weekend was the Masters Golf Tournament. The men in my family are avid golfers. We watch golf every weekend. I was eating lunch on the Saturday of the tournament and looked over into my family room.

"Look guys," I said to my husband and son, "Tiger Woods is going to win the Masters. "Yeah right!" they replied with a laugh. Tiger Woods has endured multiple injuries and surgeries, and it was the first-time playing golf after recovering from back surgery.

I said, "No, really…look!" I laid out my case based on the signs I saw from the universe. My son's report on Tiger Woods from elementary school, rediscovered by his Aunt Kathy when she came to stay with us and care for me, was lying out on the coffee table. Behind the coffee table is a red armchair with a framed picture of a hole in Augusta, Georgia at the Masters hanging above it. The red armchair is in between these two symbols connected to Tiger, because on Sunday Tiger always wears a Red Shirt.

They thought I was nuts. On Sunday while watching, I was rooting for Tiger to win. If he *can come back and win at life, so can I!* I thought. When he won, I was beyond ecstatic.

I later saw an interview with Lindsey Vonn. She said, "No one talks about the pain. The pain is a real thing. It helps us heal when we can talk about it. Not to bring someone down, it helps when letting it out of our bodies so we can visualize the light."

We take one step at a time to get there. It is not allowing distractions and the interference of other's influences to take precedence over what we want to get accomplished. Becoming non-reactionary helps you get calmer and clearer and keeps us more grounded. There is no rushing healing. It takes time to heal the body, mind, and spirit. We are expected to behave in a certain way towards pain.

After this painful journey, I have realized how important self-belief is. Until we believe in our heart and soul that we can do anything we set our minds to, nothing will ever change. Once we change our mindset to—*Yes, I can do that, I will do that!*—the shift we have been waiting for can happen.

We discover that the roadblock in our path has been self-created all along. It is about changing the impossible to *I am possible*. We are a sum of the beliefs we have carried our whole lives.

Take, for example, the writing of this book. I am *not smart enough to write and be an author of a book. There are too many steps to take to do it,* I would think. If I chose to believe those thoughts, then nothing could happen. I had to decide instead that nothing else will get in the way of focusing on doing what it takes to get it done. It made me laugh, thinking that my brain loves to go fast, that writing will go fast along with my brain, since my body was moving so slowly.

When I think and study the behaviors of leaders, they just keep moving forward. They plan, commit with dedication, and discipline themselves to accomplish the mastering of the mind. They go beyond the brain's doubt and fear. They think it into *being* not think it into doubt. *Think it. Ink it.* That became a motto of sorts for me while writing this book.

It really comes down to the adage, *how will you ever know unless you try?* That is, it in the nutshell—TRY.—Crack the shell, open, and plant the nut to discipline, commitment and focus just like athletes do. When life changes to be hard, change yourself to be stronger. Be stronger than excuses. Turn your mess into a message.

I had challenged myself like this once before, when I decided to start my own business with the last money of my mother's estate. My mother always believed in me. She told me when I was born that I was nothing like my other sisters, that I had a glow of light around me when they handed me to her. She always said

I was different than the rest. As I got older, I joked saying, "Well, I am your only kid born in a different generation!" Each generation comes in with their own thoughts, beliefs and sharing things their own way.

My mom was right that there was something different about me. Having the gifts that I have of intuition and psychic abilities, it has been tough for me emotionally to fit in. Anywhere I have been—school or work, spiritually or socially— I have always trusted God and followed His guiding light. Trusting the plans God has for us is really the only thing we can do. When we discover the true alignment of the brain and heart aligning together is where love and compassion lies for oneself, and others is the recipe for true healing within.

As time went on, approaching the one-year anniversary of my broken ankle, doing whatever it took to heal, I was back in the gym at an abdominal class. The trainer Dennis said, "Patti, you have grit." I was like, "What does that mean?"

I went home and made a Facebook post celebrating it being one year since my injury, and an advertisement came up for a pearl necklace themed around grit. That was my sign. I had to buy it, a gift for myself for coming so far.

The necklace's description said "She is unstoppable, not because she does not know pain, but because she always shows up and never gives up. Because she believes anything is possible, no matter the odds, and perhaps what makes her beautiful has less to do with what lies on the surface and more to do with what lies within. She is not just beautiful because of her appearance, NO! She is beautiful because of the way she chooses to live and love. In this way she embraces all of life's expertise. Good or Bad. In her willingness to bend but never break and in her courage to believe that the darkness cannot hold her if she continues to create her own light. She is just like a pearl—made from grit. But full of grace she is unstoppable, she knows it is not what happens but how she chooses to respond with perseverance in her mind and passion in her heart."

That was it concisely. Beyond the pain, lies the light brighter than ever because the thoughts and beliefs that the darkness brought had clearly lifted. Now, I know that I have the power to choose the light, because I have sat in the darkness and until you have, you cannot ever appreciate the light as much. These days it does not really matter to me what the weather is doing because my sunshine lies within my heart. That is where our light radiates our love deep within our soul. That is when you have become the victor in your race for victory over the darkness.

We can be that warrior princess when we decide what the fears are that block our light. Having been hit hard from PTSD after the ankle break, I know mentally I had to overcome the fear that created the fear, or that fear would continue to have a hold on me until I did.

Before my injury and the healing journey I subsequently embarked on, I never understood all the elements it takes to accomplish what you want to achieve. I now know that success is not measured by things we accumulate, which are so often a waste of time we spend trying to impress others.

Instead, my success will be measured in being able to walk normally, run normally, and in being able to return to the adventures I love to do. It is always great to see the views from the top of beautiful mountains. The landscape of our world is a beautiful place. We just need to get outside and see it. I have spent tremendous time this year taking in the trees from my deck, just sitting there doing absolutely nothing. Really. Nothing. No thoughts. Just staring and focusing on the trees, the birds, bugs, squirrels, hawks, enjoying the sound of the wind, the beautiful breeze and of course the beautiful SUN.

I really feel like I was rescued from going six feet under. This journey made me realize it was really my soul that needed rescuing. I have really loved and enjoyed spending time with my friends and family, going on lunch dates. I joke all the time how I do not have time to work because "I do lunch!"—Ha, ha!—I have worked my whole life, and it sure has been fun sleeping in until I get up.

I have enjoyed going to the gym when I want, taking naps on my deck during the summer, soaking up the sunshine, blue skies, enjoying the sounds of nature and animals, the calming wind rustling through the trees, having a glass of wine during the day because your girlfriend just stops over for a visit.

I have enjoyed finally allowing myself to ask and have my needs met. It truly feels so good. I have felt my powerful sense of intuition get stronger and my clairvoyance increase. I would love to see them both continue to increase. I have loved just taking things at my own pace, enjoying the quiet mornings, listening to the sounds of nature, and feeling the breeze. I feel less annoyed, more peaceful, less responsible.

Always wanting to help others understand and seek the light, to experience the joy that life has in it. I prayed to God so much to help me see what this was all about. One night, lying there all alone in the dark and quiet, I heard *How else can you really know what the light is unless you have experienced being in the dark yourself?*

My healing journey gave me a stronger level of compassion for myself and others that are living with so much pain. We all need love and compassion. We never know the plans for our lives, we just trust the process of whatever is asked of us to do or be participants in. Engulfed with anger and judgment just wastes our precious energy and keeps us off track of our beauty. Our goal is to spread love and light and trusting in the process is a beautiful plan. Learning all the gifts and staying focused to live life on purpose is a beautiful thing.

Started collaborating with an orthopedic personal trainer in the area. After a couple of appointments, he asked how my injury happened and why was Utah listed on my chart. I told him my story. He then asked when I was going to travel back to see my son.

"Next year," I replied.

"Why are you going to wait until then before you'll visit?" he said.

He suggested going sooner than later because all it does is delay it further. He said, by my next appointment he wanted an airplane ticket booked. Making the decision to visit my son was easy. It was the idea of hiking over snow that was a whole different level of hard!

After hitting the "book" button for my flight, I started getting very anxious about going. I had to gear myself up by counting the days before the flight. The night before, I was not able to sleep because I was so anxious. The morning of the flight I was trying to get a grip on what it would be like when I got there.

As I got off the plane my entire body was completely engulfed with a tremendous amount of emotion. My heart was pumping a mile a minute. *Wondering, Can I do this? Is it too soon? Am I really healed? Will it be safe to hike?*

As I was waiting for my son's girlfriend to pick me up from the airport, I was standing there waiting when this tall, handsome man came towards me. Mind you, I am the one that usually cuts my son's hair. His hair was long, so I did not recognize him as my son until he said, "Hi Mom!" It was a surprise that he picked me up when I was expecting his girlfriend to pick me up. As I was hugging him, my anxiety started getting calmer. I was proud of myself for being there. Conquering that first hurdle felt good.

One of the activities planned for my visit was going to join my son at his work. He works in the adaptive sports rehabilitation program at the University of Utah Hospital and Clinic. The adaptive program was created and designed to specialize in assisting those with complex disabilities and/or physical injuries to be able to partake in the activities that they love.

The morning, I went with him was very emotional. There was a tremendous amount of snow in Utah, so I knew what was coming—walking over that snow. There had been truly little snow back home in Cincinnati during the winter following my ankle break, so I was especially apprehensive about having to walk over snow for the first time.

When we got to the ski resort that the adaptive sports rehabilitation program uses, I had the opportunity to meet the people that my son serves in the program. I met Barry,

who was ejected, and completely thrown out of a truck during an accident, paralyzing the left side of his body and leaving him with little mobility. He is a man of true courage and strength. He entered the program wanting to learn how to ski again with two feet. As he was talking to me telling me his story, he started to have tears in his eyes. It was so powerful to hear and feel this man's journey to recover.

Another man, Dave, who had suffered a stroke and became paralyzed also on his left side of his body. I met his wife, Chris, who is so patient and kind. She was telling me their daily challenges that he must overcome. What a struggle for these people that they endure just to do life every day. It made me cry and be very emotional for hours on end watching them get into a specialized device, called a Tetra Ski, to be able to ski down the mountain. I kept crying thinking of their lives and the challenges they must overcome just to do this one thing.

They both knew about my broken ankle recovery and offered love and healing. It was utterly amazing to receive such a gift of love and compassion from ones that have endured way more challenges. It was so healing to be around people who intimately know the intensity of debilitating pain. Words to describe other people's pain is not an easy task. We often bury our pain deep within ourselves just to show a better side of ourselves to people, wearing masks of fake smiles just to make others happy.

But deep within are layers upon layers of deep excruciating raw pain. With every minute of our lives, we choose whether to just deal with it or to do the work to discover what causes the traumas of the pain. Real healing takes one step at a time. We have so many options at our disposal. Drugs to numb the pain, or a multitude of other modalities that can assist us in the discovery of balancing our bodies once we release what is causing the pain.

To be a true warrior we must have courage, perseverance, and determination. There is a feeling of true freedom when we can overcome despair and heartache. We become challenged with the true comeback story within. Everyone has the bravery to take that step forward and face the fear that holds them locked up in pain. True triumph comes from facing what we fear head on, otherwise the fear will have a grip on us forever. Getting to the level of feeling true peace, love, and joy is what our souls are trying to attain.

All resistance to surrender will lead you on a course of action that needs to unfold, to finally free yourself of the fear of extremely tough stuff. Keeping focused on the result of the feeling keeps me going. Coming out of the shade into the light. Getting out of the head that has a different language. Deleting all the chatter in our heads, into the higher frequency of creating something new. I strive to have a drive of passion from the heart and mind as one in unison together, that beats as one.

I want more than anything to have that feeling inside and offer it to others with truth, love, respect, compassion, and honor with peace in my heart. To have love, we must have peace. That is where love lies with the heart. It is where all of us get stuck wanting to close it off to protect ourselves from further pain. But that only robs us of our joy, peace, and true love of heart! The art of love rises higher.

We lower our vibration of light to try to fit into a vibration that understands us. Then we spend and waste so much energy trying to prove and justify our viewpoint and match that energy of vibration. This creates an energy of frustration, anger, and hate because that energy does not understand us. Then we live in doubt, fear, and unworthiness. That is where we get stuck so many times, if we feel it is not permissible and not allowed in society to be our true selves. The root cause of pain is that we give so much of our power to insecurities.

When confidence and courage awaken to finally believe in yourself, trust yourself, know yourself, that knowingness allows you to trust your gut, and listen to your intuition that guides us. To make clear decisions, we must choose faith over fear! We believe in our hearts and souls we have the world in our hands to go forth and be who we are created to be.

A Pearl Made From Grit
Reflection Questions

1. Do you live in the light of positivity, or do you find yourself entrapped by negative thoughts?

2. Do you push yourself to know how strong you are? Do you celebrate your wins no matter how big or small?

3. Do athletes' stories inspire you?

4. How disciplined are you in getting things accomplished? What do you do when you encounter a roadblock?

5. Are you aware each generation brings innovative ideas and beliefs to the world? What differences have you noticed between the generations?

6. Do you feel comfortable asking others for your needs to be met?

7. How well do you trust your intuition?

SPIRAL JETTY

During a later trip to Utah, we made a visit to the Spiral Jetty in Corinne, Utah.

The sculpture is designed and constructed like a labyrinth. The artist who sculpted it wanted to create a transcendent theme, an imposed unnatural form that succumbed to inexorable natural power of the changing conditions of the surrounding water, land, and atmosphere. The artist's vision was for visitors to wish for whatever they desire as they walk through the maze.

As I was walking through the spiral, I reflected on what a journey this has been the last few years. I began to compose a visual upward spiral and the understanding of belief and trust that God is the true artist in our lives. Weaving lessons, showing us signs and wonders on our beautiful paths. Every place, every person I met on this journey of transcendence was a theme of artistry orchestrated with alignment of a much larger power than myself. What better beauty to witness God's hands in showing and invoking a much greater appreciation of learning to be more compassionate, calmer, wiser, and the true gift of a deeper spiritual self, all created and woven by God. Teaching me how to be resilient and persevere my strength into a pearl made from grit. A true gift in and of itself.

We were climbing up the mountain which consisted of shale and loose rocks. I was very apprehensive about climbing up due to the unstable ground. I became extremely anxious. My son reached out his hand and said, "Mom, I got you!"

I stood straight up to balance my footing, and replied, "No thank you, I'm good." As I claimed that thought, in that moment I heard the small voice in my head say, *Every person for themself!* That was truly a gift to learn to think quickly on my feet, stand my ground, stand up for myself, stand on my own two feet! The power that came over me was amazing!

The next day, we took a day trip to visit the Bonneville Salt Flats. I was riding in the back seat of my son's truck and my son, and his girlfriend were listening to a podcast called, "Out Alive." The podcast interviews people about their outdoor survival stories, how they had gotten injured along the way, and their rescue stories.

I really wanted to tell my son and girlfriend, "Shut that fucking thing off!" It was really triggering me on my long-standing PTSD, and the ride was about two and a half hours each way. Instead, I did not say a word. At first, I just tried to drown it out. But after a while, I found myself listening. It was the story of a woman sharing her experience with getting trapped under an avalanche. She had broken her leg and was unable to move until rescue workers came to her aid and dug her out.

She talked about how her PTSD and severe pain had her stuck for years. She shared about not having any joy and being unable to experience anyone else's joy for years. She wondered if she would ever experience joy again. She explained that she would tell her story repeatedly and it seemed like people were getting tired of hearing about it. She thought to herself, *I am still in it.*

It takes a tremendous amount of mental and physical energy to bring yourself out of the darkness. During Christmas time five years after her accident, one day she woke up and felt the joy re-enter into her whole being. She said to herself, "I'm not broken, I'm just different."

My whole body shifted in thinking, *that is it!* That is the piece of the puzzle I was searching for, and I so needed to hear her speak it. *No longer broken, just different.* My body and soul were whole again. Filled with pure joy, the last piece of PTSD just lifted right off after hearing her story. It was as if it is okay to give yourself permission to release it to allow the joy and love to re-enter in again.

Realizing I had been trapped in my own emotional trauma for so long, without knowing how to get out of it, I just stayed in a dark place. This experience has truly been transformative, in knowing and trusting myself at a completely different level of awareness. Isolation and feeling trapped in pain caused me to close my heart off to love and joy. Pain created such anger at the core of my being, darkening all my thoughts. Getting me further and further from the light! Being trapped in pain. I needed to find my own way to the love, light, and joy again. Unless I did, it would haunt me and keep me from feeling the freedom to live as the free spirit I am. Every day I wake up I know it is an opportunity to make a choice! Finally feeling I want to live to the fullest. Being in love with life again!

Spiral Jetty Reflection Questions

1. What have you learned about other people's challenges and how they overcome them?

2. What type of warrior do you believe you are?

3. Are you open or resistant to seeking the answers about your own challenges?

4. If things trigger you, do you speak up and express your emotions and feelings about it?

   _____

   _____

   _____

5. Have you given permission to yourself to let go and release things that no longer serve you for your highest good?

   _____

   _____

   _____

6. Do you take time to reflect?

   _____

   _____

   _____

7. Do you love life and enjoy simple things? Do you live with a grateful heart?

   _____

   _____

   _____

Acknowledgements

I thank God for his love and guiding light! My invisible friend, yet so visible and powerful!

Father Ruffino, thank you for sharing the best advice and healing.

To my mom and dad, who instilled good values, wisdom, and taught me to have respect for myself and others. Your strength and love continue to live in me.

To my oldest sister Laurie, my bookend of light, who continues to shine her light on me in the afterlife. Her love and patience guided me through all the term papers in school. God, I Love and miss you so much!

To my husband George, thank you for your love, kindness, extreme patience, sense of humor and unwavering support. You are such an unbreakable rock! I Love you!

To my sons, George, and Austin, who have taught me more about life and how to live it with excitement and enthusiasm in my soul. I thank you from the bottom of my heart for all you do and continue to teach me. I love you to the moon and back!

To my daughter-in-law Sarah, thank you for your love and joyfulness, you are fiercely independent and always reminding me that true strength lies within. Love you!

Taylor, thank you for your sincere compassion from the heart, and your gentle caring and kindness. Thank you for the adult coloring books and colored pencils to keep me occupied during my recovery. Love you!

Kota bear, you truly are such an amazing dog! You're always willing to join in on any adventure that just adds to the fun and excitement. You really are DOG spelled backwards. Thank you for lending me your leash. Love you!

Ruby Rye, grand pup, you are such a healing and lovely addition to the family. Who shares her cuteness and love. Love you!

The Goblin Valley helpers who emerged from the earth. You were truly a blessing of love, faith and trusting to believe in miracles. Raquel, Josh, Theresa, Jessica, Christian Stevens, Chandler Hyer, Julia Hammond, Catherine Summers. My sincere gratitude to all of you for giving of yourselves to help others in such a time of need. Thank you, does not even cover it!! Love and appreciation to all of you!!

Thank you to nurse Nancy, from the insurance company. Your guidance on what to do was incredibly helpful.

The ER staff at The University of Utah Hospital. Thank you for the exceptional care!! From the minute we arrived to upon leaving. Even followed up the next day. This hospital is in a class all by itself!

Thank you, Delta Airlines, the flight attendant Becky, and staff were beyond attentive and made it so comforting. Thank you especially to the pilot! A-1 on flying a smooth flight.

The wheelchair assistants at Salt Lake City and Cincinnati airports.

The gentlemen who deboarded last and stopped to offer well wishes of hope.

Thank you to my sisters Debi and Kathy, and friend Fiona who were the first to call and offer their love and healing. The three of them had experienced a similar break. They knew the road ahead and offered great love and compassion.

Thank you to Beacon Orthopedics and Sports Medicine, for your unwavering dedication and the positive impact you made! Dr. Adam Miller, Mark, and dedicated staff assistants. Appreciate everything you did and then some!

Thank you to Carrie, April, Susie, Michael, and Bob for taking excellent care of the clients.

Thank you to my sister-in-law Lou for purchasing Kathy's flight. Thank you, Kathy, for the Royal treatment of nurturing and the best care giver anyone can ask for. Sincere gratitude to both of you. Love you!

Thank you to my cousin Bonnie for her love and continued support of phone calls during the writing of this book. Love you!

Thank you to the wonderful ladies who taught the art of lunch dates! Incredibly fun! Sandy, Teri,

Susie, Cathy, Kate, Julie, Terry, Peggy, Mei Mei, my niece Katie, and her sweet newborn daughter Eleanor. Enjoyed all of you, much appreciation. What a treat to do Lunch. Love you!

To all my friends and clients who offered texts, phone calls of comfort, visits, gifts, and delicious meals. Teri, Teri Lynn, Paul, Mindy, Marci, Kate, Katie, Karen, Marian, Tracy, Susie, Beth, Carol, Joan, Ted, Mike, Heidi, Ann, Cathy, John, CeCe, Katherine, Michele, Anne, David, Tamara, Dawson, Marion, Michelle, Breck, Susan, Sudie, Sue, Dan, Lynn, Marty, Reed, Dale, Laura, Mary Kate, Carrie, Doug, Evelyn, Jeff, Rob, Barb, Jeannie, Adam, and Megan. Thank you! You all added bright sunshine and truly touched my heart! Beyond grateful to you! Love You!

To my dear friend Patty, who made delicious feasts every Monday for many months. The High School musical, Mary Poppins. Coffee dates, slushy, trip to the Nature Center to just sit under the trees and enjoy the sunshine. Thank you, to you, your daughter Kristen, and husband Chris! Much appreciation and beyond gratefulness! Love you!

Thank you, Carol, and Joan, for your friendship and the fun trip to Carol's beach house! Joan, you were such a trooper pushing the wheelchair through the airports. You both were so loving and patient during the trip. Especially the fun establishments and surprises along the way. Love you!

A special extension of gratitude to Teri Lynn and Paul. Your generosity is beyond words!! Your gentle nudges of support and unwavering love of friendship are so appreciated! Thank you, I Love you!

Thank you, Barry, Dave, and Chris, for your example of true bravery, inspiration, and compassion. So, appreciate you!

Thank you to Lindsey Vonn and Tiger Woods for your true dedication of excellence to be a high-performance athlete. You're a great example of what it takes to overcome the impossible to possible! Appreciate you both very much!

To all the clients who have sat in my salon, and coaching chairs over the years, you have enriched my life far more than you can imagine. Thank you!

Thank you, Jeannie, and Jan, for the use of the shower chair, transport, and walker.

A special thank you to Dana and Donna at Country Fresh Produce Market for getting the order of groceries ready for pick up.

Thank you to the spiritual advisors, Thomas Windlow, Lisa Gerard, Diane Emira, Alecia Caine and Annie in Sedona, Arizona.

Thank you to my two neighbors Yianni and Elizabeth for the great inspirational conversations and continued support. Love You!

Thank you, Phillip Rosenthal, for creating the show "Somebody Feed Phil". You provided the best entertainment for the long recovery. The places you go are incredibly entertaining to see. I thoroughly enjoyed it, especially laughing along with you and the crew!

Thank you to the Conduits for Healing, Blu Fries, Sally Oyler Gehlert, Sue McLaughlin, Toby Christianson, Anne Stephan Russo, Eric Russo, Natalie Mckerral, Susie Oneil, Tara Metzger, and Dr. Brain H Duermit. Your commitment to your profession and gifts are exceptional! I am truly grateful to all of you! Love you!

Thank you to the Physical Therapists, Johnathon, Jeff, Sam, Dawn and Rocky. Whose guidance of expertise, and extreme patience are extraordinary. Appreciate everything you all did!

Thank you to Anderson Mercy Health Plex staff, and the club members for inspiration. Johnathon, Dennis, Terri, Amy, Zack, Jack, Steve, Jim, Jenny, Kathy, Marilyn, Rita, Steve, Ben, Christy, Sue, Cindy, Perry, Sydney, Jill, and Deanna. You all have empowered the comeback story! Incredibly grateful to all your compassion and love. Love you guys!

To my trainer Dennis Cloud, for your exceptional knowledge, your strength, compassion, and encouragement to go the distance. For your emotional support on those days, you just don't have the energy emotionally or physically. For when your spirit is so low you just want to give up and throw in the towel. You always give it your all! Thank you especially for being in tune and aware of the look on my face when I carried that vacant stare.

You not only knew from experience that look, but you also knew what it felt like deep within the soul. Knowing PTSD is no joke! From the bottom of my heart, I thank you!! Appreciate you more than you will ever know!

Thank you, Mindy, for your special friendship and love! The shopping trips to buy a bathing suit and push the wheelchair around the store and maneuver it around in the dressing room, OH the laughs we had! For creating the most beautiful heart for the cover of the book. Your talent for artwork is so exceptional! Appreciate you so much! I Love you!

Thank you, Ze, from Staples, you were so helpful. Appreciate your assistance at the last minute.

Thank you, Mary Kate, for your patience in typing the first draft and translating it from the messy handwriting. Thank you for the years of friendship and support. You are such an inspiration! Love you!

Thank you to Rees Strom and M.J. for your brilliant skills and organization of edits. You ladies were so encouraging and extremely helpful and patient. As both of you know this is not an easy task. With your assistance you really were the reason this project came to completion. With my sincere gratitude I thank you! Love you both!

Thank you to the Today Show cast, you guys "ROCK" the universe at Rockefeller Plaza. You all sure know how to instill a great laugh for the morning coffee. That is a true gift of healing. Appreciate all the work you do day in and day out!

Thank you to all these talented musicians for creating the most inspirational music. Music can really help aid in healing! My healing mantra songs: Help-The Beatles, Shower the people with Love-James Taylor, The Climb-Miley Cyrus, Fight Song-Rachel Platten, I Send You Out-John Angotti, Walking on Sunshine-Katrina & The Waves, Come Monday-Jimmy Buffet, Break My Stride-Matthew Wilder, Rascal Flats-Life is a Highway, Dancing on the Ceiling-Lionel Richie, Dancing Queen-Abba, Unstoppable-Sia, Photograph-Ed Sheeran, I Believe- Josh Groban, Don't Stop Believin-Journey, Shallow-Lady Gaga & Bradley Cooper, Roar and Firework-Katy Perry, Girl on Fire-Alicia Keys, Thunderstruck-ACDC, All Star-Smash Mouth, True Colors-Cyndi Lauper, Shake It Off-Taylor Swift, Chariots Of Fire-Vangelis, Eye Of The Tiger-Survivor, I'm A Survivor-Reba McEntire, Heal The World-Michael Jackson, Turn the lights Back On-Billy Joel, Brave-Sara Bareilles, Broken and Beautiful-Kelly Clarkson.

Thank you to the staff of Buckeye Running and Fleet Feet Stores in Cincinnati, Ohio, for fitting the perfect gym shoes for the healing comeback. "Hoka's" are my recommendation!! They are like walking on sunshine and marshmallows!

A special thank you to all the talent and expertise at Luminare Press-Self-Publishing Company. You all were so incredible to work with and always seemed to know exactly what I was thinking, and you all implemented it so seamlessly. Grateful for your exceptional work!

*"The real purpose of running isn't to win the race,
It's to test the limits of the human heart."*

—Coach Bill Bowerman
University of Oregon Coaching legend

"Even in the darkest of days the sun always shines."

/pod-product-compliance

3/3665